Katherine Burger

THE BILDUNGSROMAN
OF
MR. BOB

A Cat's Tale

THE BILDUNGSROMAN OF MR. BOB

A Cat's Tale

An Illustrated Novella for Adults

by KATHERINE BURGER

Dr. Cicero Books

Designed by Abigail Sturges

Dr. Cicero Books
New York Rio de Janeiro Paris
First Edition
Manufactured in the United States of América
ISBN-13: 978-1-945766-27-5

DEDICATION

⇜　⇝

This book is dedicated
to the memory of the original Bobcat,
a singular cat who shared my life.

Contents

༄   ༄

The Dark Unconscious Floats Beneath

Early Memories

❧ ❧

I did not come into my own, my true nature, my ur-self until I was on the verge of my second year, when, as I will relate to you, dear reader, a change in circumstance revealed to me both the heart of dark desire where instinct reigns, and a higher self of proportion and probity. I contain, as the poet said, multitudes.

When young we are pure id. As we grow older we gain, in varying degrees, wisdom, reason, empathy for others. Yet the dark unconscious floats unseen beneath the calm waters of our seeming selves, honing its teeth and flexing its thick antediluvian limbs. We are uneasy swimmers in the sea of life. I will not, however, prevail upon your patience any longer with metaphysical metaphors, but will commence forthwith the story of my formative early life, my bildungs-roman, if you will, and in time-honored tradition endeavor to show rather than explain how I have grappled with the conundrum known as instinct for the duration up till now.

Nature Stirred In Us

Of my infancy the merest sketch will suffice. My earliest memories are of the usual jumble of warm sibling bodies – six of us squirming for an available teat, nestling and breathing in unison. We were at first one being; we slept and ate and slept as one. Nature stirred in us, however; soon we were crawling, standing up on shaky legs, falling, lurching forward, falling again, frisking, scampering, gamboling, cavorting, climbing, prevailing. I grew, I flourished, I learned to eat solid food, both wet and dry. "Feline Growth" it said upon the can, and I endeavored to fulfill its promised outcome.

The huge creature who walked on his hind legs was there from the beginning – a human. At first all I could apprehend was hands, naked and furless. The creature talked to us, and sometimes sang, I suppose, because he could not purr. He sat in a big chair and let us climb all over him, up to his lap, his shoulders, and his furry head.

The day my own human came into my life began as any other. I woke up, stretched, and yowled for food. I chased my tail and those of my two sisters. I skittered sideways across the linoleum, back arched and tail inflated, because the sunlight shifted in the room. I slept, then scaled an armchair to the kitchen counter and ate a half a stick of butter.

A new creature came into the room. Her name was Laura – I heard the other human call her that. The fur on her head was longer than that of the male creature. Her body was smaller and had a different shape. Her voice was more melodious than his, with a tremolo just verging on a purr. She let me smell her hand before she picked me up. She had a yellow scent, sweet and salt, like butter.

"What a beautiful kitten! He looks just like a little lynx, a bobcat. Those markings! Those cushy paws! What a plumy tail he has! That face, that lilac colored nose, those deep green eyes!" This was the first inkling I had that I am, through no effort of my own, a handsome cat. False modesty is a coy pose given such undeniable beauty as my own.

"Would you like to come and live with me?" she asked. My own mother had begun to thrust me from her breast. This creature had a soothing voice and a reassuring smell; she knew how to scratch just so behind my ears. I leaped at the chance, right into Laura's lap, and so sealed my feline fate.

She Let Me Smell Her Hand

DOGS

Enormous Changes

❧ ❧

I Go On A Journey

Things got unpleasant then. I was thrust into a nylon bag, hoisted aloft, and carried beyond the boundaries of my known world. The smells changed, the noise increased, the swaying made me giddy. The view through the bag's mesh window was too alarming to incorporate into my limited worldview. Stairs, streets, people, buses, DOGS – I burrowed into a corner of the bag and wept.

Eventually I began to purr. Human beings have the wrong idea that purring cats are happy cats. Not always so. We purr when we're content, it's true, but also when distraught. (The first sound I heard was my mother purring as I came into the world – although perhaps this is more a sentimental conceit than a true memory.) Purring. Just say the word to yourself, reflectively rolling the r's. You see what a soothing sound it is. The sensation itself –

deep within the very fiber of our feline selves – is one of profound soothingness and calm. It is a tranquilizer when we are agitated, a statement of our deep content when life is good. And so I purred, hoping that what I believe is life's essential goodness would once more envelop me with sunshine, warm windowsills, soft nests, and ample food, both wet and dry.

I swayed and bumped and purred. The sounds and smells of the outside world whipped through my senses like ribbons of harsh bright colors, and still I purred. I purred until I was in some kind of trance. And then the movement stopped. A zipper opened in the nylon roof above my head, and Laura lifted me into my new home.

Laura

I will spare you the painstaking account of how I poked my lilac nose into each corner of my new abode. It seemed so vast at first. I was frightened of these unknown rooms that had no smell of cat. I crept from the nylon bag to the nearest piece of furniture and scuttled underneath. Laura reached under and dragged me, hissing and protesting, back into the light. She insisted on showing me my own personal litter tray, and bowls of food and water in another room. All I wanted was to crawl under something and cry for my mother to come and rescue me but Laura followed me from room to room, pulling me from my hiding places.

She finally left me alone and disappeared. I needed to use the litter box and found my way back there, hugging the walls en route. The litter box room was dark and cool. I sidled inside and stepped cautiously into the litter tray. (What is it in our natures, I wondered, that instructs us to bury our excrement in the sand? What is this pre-existing knowledge known as instinct? Even in extremis I had a penchant for the metaphysical.) After I had accomplished my objective I noticed an enormous metal thing perched on four clawed feet clutching round orbs. I put my front paws on its side and stretched up, peering into its interior, for it was hollow, a shell. At one end a shiny metal snout dripped water, which puddled on the bottom of the thing. It was a giant water dish! I inched my way underneath, until I reached a corner of the wall. I huddled against it and waited, for what I don't know. After a while I tried purring again but the sound echoed and rattled back at me in a metallic clangor. Spooked, I ran out from underneath the giant dish, and out of the room of cold, slick surfaces. I crept along the hallway wall, to the living room. It was empty. The windows were filled with night and I with loneliness.

I had never been alone before. The Laura creature puzzled me. I didn't know if she was friend or foe; she had taken me away from my known world. But she was another living being, and I went looking for her. Kitchen, hallway – she was nowhere to be found. I climbed up the stairs, resting on each step, and emerged at their summit to find Laura lying on a big soft rectangle.

"You can come up on the bed," she said, "It's all right." I climbed up the bedspread and lay down as far as possible from her. She started to reach for me. I inflated all my fur and wrinkled my nose at her. She withdrew her hand. "Good night then, Mr. Bob" she said and went to sleep. So, eventually, did I.

The Table Was No-Place-For-Cats

In the morning I found that I was lying against her feet. The following morning I woke up curled in the crook of her knees. By the week's end I slept curled up by her shoulder and suffered her to rub my belly when I stretched.

From tolerance came habituation; habituation nurtured affection; affection grew to love. I came to love Laura, with all the joy, irritation, bemusement, and serenity that signify true love.

Sometimes she was difficult to train; she'd gush and coo and want to hold me in her lap when it was inconvenient to my sensibilities. She wanted me to come when called, and had an absurd idée fixee that the table was No-Place-For-Cats when interesting things were placed upon it – food, knitting, board games of any kind. She didn't seem to understand how utterly misguided she was in this conceit, no matter how often I demonstrated my avid interest in the tabletop at crucial moments. Speaking of food: she seemed to think I liked my Feline Growth. All right, I did. But that did not preclude a taste for other food – roast chicken, melon, the milk and sugar left when the granola's gone.

And yet, and yet. At times I was in helpless thrall to her. Whenever she came home from her mysterious absences outside I'd be there like a fool, rolled over on my back, my furry tummy aching for her touch. I couldn't sleep at night until I'd spent some moments pouncing on her feet or crawling through the caverns formed by blankets and her knees. At odd moments I'd be overcome with deep and passionate emotion; I'd seek her out, climb in her lap, burrow my head against her body and purr so hard my whiskers shook.

She called me Mr. Bob, Bobcat, The Bobster, Bob, Roberto, Oh Furry Footed One, Little One One, You Monster, Cattiwampus, Mugwump, Big Guy, Kitten, and quite simply, Cat.

My Realm, Of Which I Am Undisputed Lord,
And My Amusements There

In human terms, my new home consisted of a living room, hallway, kitchen, bathroom, a mysterious closed door, and a stairway leading to a slope-ceilinged bedroom with a skylight of pebbled glass which trembled with reflections on full moon nights. There were various features I found particularly felicitous for felid purposes: a sofa with an ever changing arrangement of pillows; a bookcase whose top shelf (Alcott to Chaucer) offered a vantage point onto the entire living room and down the hall; and, most alluring and sirenic: two windows in the living room framing an Edenic paradise: a Tree of Heaven, with pigeons.

Birds. Why do they affect me as they do? Again, that strange tide turning in my brain. I see a bird and am instantly on high alert. I crouch with every nerve spring-loaded, and utter an involuntary, clicking cry: "Eh eh eh eh eh. . ."

The pigeons laughed at me: "Try and catch us – use your feathers darling." They'd open up their nacreous grey wings, plummet from the windowsill and glide to the ailanthus tree, then strut and mock me from its boughs.

Instinct grabbed me hard one day when Laura brought home a simple toy, some twists of cardboard fastened to a length of wire. She jounced it through the air and I was helpless to resist. In a frenzy I leaped after my prey. I knew it wasn't flesh and blood, winged insect, bird; I saw the wire, Laura's handling of it, but instinct surged in me to leap and grapple with a wraith. That simple construct of

A Tree Of Heaven, With Pigeons

cardboard and wire became my boon amusement. By leaping on one end of its curved length, I could cause the other end to rise and wiggle in the air. Then I'd pounce, grab it by the throat and drag my prey into my lair under the sofa. Or so I liked to make believe.

One night Laura made a clicking noise with something in her hand and a piece of furniture started talking, and moving things appeared on its vertical flat surface. I admit I jumped back.

"Don't be afraid," said Laura (I was *startled*. There is a difference). "It's just the television."

For a few nights I was mesmerized by the flickering shapes and bursts of sound, but after a while it all began to seem very much the same. Laura continued to watch it intently from time to time, although I could never interest her in watching birds. I'd sit on the windowsill and utter plaintive hunting cries, tilting my head in the most fetching manner, to no avail. They're inscrutable, humans.

Sometimes other humans came to visit Laura, singly or in groups, and this was usually a pleasant break in our routine, as most of them made a fuss over my good looks and winsome ways. Often they brought things for the table (No place for cats! No place for cats!) and some of them would slip me luscious morsels from their plates. Sometimes they all would sit upon the sofa and raptly gaze upon the moving screen, as if mesmerized en masse. Inscrutable, as I've said.

Sometimes they brought their offspring along. I quickly found out that the very young were loud and sticky but relatively inert. The older ones were unpredictable, however, and quick. I learned to retreat to the top of the bookshelf when they appeared, where I maintained a disinterested yet dignified surveillance.

I noticed that humans often came in pairs, mostly male and female, and these couples were alternately friendly to each other and not. If they'd been especially affectionate Laura would hold me after they had gone and tell me "You're my guy, Bobcat; you're my Bob." And she'd sigh, and press me close to her.

One room in the apartment was always closed. Laura would enter this room and close the door behind her. I scratched and mewed until one day she let me in. Books sagged on shelves, and spilled out onto tables and a desk. Papers lay in seeming disarray upon the table and the floor. Colorful boxes containing elongated metal spirals, chewy rubber loops, and other small items sat on the desk. Laura sat in a chair facing the desk, in front of a kind of television, her hands moving rapidly up and down on a device with rows of tiny hard pillows, which clicked up and down under her fingers.

Here is fun, thought I, and jumped up on the desk. I swatted a ceramic box and sent its contents flying.

"No," Laura said, and bent to pick things up. I put my paw on one of the little pillows, which depressed in a thoroughly satisfying way. And then I fdkltrh-vf"gjaosfbewerojk ;rk,edwf54y79-

"NO." Laura picked me up and put me on a chair. "I'm working," she admonished. Very well, I could work as well. I set to work on a pile of papers on the carpet. "NO NO NO!" Laura explained further. We enacted variations on this scene several times before I realized she was serious about keeping her playthings to herself. Lest you think this stance of hers ungenerous, let me assure you I did not judge her harshly; we make allowances for those we love. I looked on it as a quirk, a charming petulance. Perhaps she was deprived when young.

Writers Through The Ages Have
Acknowledged Their Affinity With Us

Eventually I consented to sit with her in companionable silence while she played – excuse me, worked – with her desk toys. There was a window in the office which looked out on a different vista than the living room: the street. People, trucks, cars, and dogs moved below me in ever-changing patterns and I would gaze down, fascinated, on this fluid scenario while Laura peered intently at her own, smaller realm. These times of silent companionship had a deep resonance for me. Sometimes I think I felt our bond most strongly in these moments of separate togetherness.

Often in the evenings she read aloud to me. Sometimes it was to share a particular bon mot or touching sentiment, sometimes she read to more deeply understand a favorite writer's cadences. (Dickens we both loved!) In this way my education was enlarged beyond the ken of many, but not all, cats. Writers through the ages have acknowledged their affinity with us; think of all the authors' photos on the back of tomes: tableaux vivants of bookcase, coffee cup, pipe, grave-faced author and feline friend.

Think Of All The Authors' Photos On The Back Of Tomes

Eat, Play, Love

This was the compass of my life: eat, play, love – and sleep. I adjusted my schedule to Laura's. She came and went, leaving me alone for hours at a time. Where did she go? At first I thought she stayed in the hallway outside the front door; I had no conception of the wider world. But then I saw her from the front office window walking down the street – so small, foreshortened and impersonal, but clearly her, my Laura. And moments later there she was, footsteps on the stairs, key in the lock, herself, her greeting, her hand upon my proffered belly.

But where did she go, and why? For a while I tried to stop her leaving, weaving myself between her legs and meowing in a poignant voice.

"I'm sorry, but I have to go and earn that 'Feline Growth'" she said one day, and I understood then that this was her form of hunting, to don uncomfortable looking clothes and foray out onto the street.

Routine

Cats thrive on routine. I woke at the same time every morning, and trotted downstairs to watch Laura take her shower. The gush of water from the faucet never ceases to amaze; the drip when it's turned off is likewise mesmerizing. I tried to show her how to wash herself, but have given up. I know when I'm licked (if you'll indulge a vulgar parlance), just as I know she'll never by her own tongue be (if you'll forgive both uses of the word). For one thing, she wasn't limber enough; I saw her do her stretches. At least she tried. After our stretches I watched her dress, then led the way to breakfast, nose up and tail alert. We dined, and it was good.

Each day was spent variously, and yet within comfortable parameters of the known. Five minutes batting a rolled-up sock across the floor; a twenty minute nap on top of the TV; a visit to the thunder box, celebrated by ten seconds of broken field running at top speed; three minutes' contemplation of an ant's slow progress along a countertop before I ate him up; a long and dream-drenched sleep draped across a pillow like an odalisque; an hour each at windows front and back, a dry food snack, a nap, a nap, and yet another nap.

In dreams I seemed to find another self. Small rituals of blood and death enthralled, intimations of things I'd never done disturbed my private slumber. In dreams my eyes would reflect the moon; my claws unsheathe; I'd let out a liquid hunting cry – then I'd wake up, embarrassed as though I had revealed too much.

Contemplation Of An Ant's Slow Progress

The Overhead Lights Went Off

More Changes,
Both Natural and Not

❧   ❧

An Unpleasant Occurence

One day I had an urge to urinate not in my box but on the yellow bath-mat. The odor was strong and strangely pleasing to my olfactory sensibilities. I conceived a plan to mark all furniture with my stink; it seemed a suddenly compelling necessity. This is my space, my dominion and my realm. Smell of my piss, you rivals, and despair!

"Uh oh," said Laura, when she came home, "I guess it's time."

She put me back in the nylon bag with the mesh front and carried me out the door, down the stairs and through the streets, despite my vociferous protestations that I was not enjoying this. We came to a place that reeked of harsh, astringent smells. Laura spoke to a woman wearing a white jacket, a sartorial choice I'd never seen on Laura or her friends. I caught a few words – anesthesia, incision, suture – which I did not understand, but which aroused in me the gravest apprehension. Laura peered at me through the mesh.

"Good-bye Bobster. I'll see you soon." And then she handed me to the stranger. I heard her steps clicking away, a door open and close. "Good-bye"? What did she mean? Then again, she'd said "I'll see you soon." What did that mean, "soon"? It certainly didn't mean a few minutes, as these came and went.

I was carried to a room full of stacked boxes made of latticed metal. These held animals – cats and dogs. I could smell their fear. The woman handed me to a white-coated man and he put me in one of these prisons. Its floor was covered with torn newspaper, though I could feel the iron mesh beneath. The man and woman then opened and closed all the boxes, placing food inside and removing soiled paper.

"No food for number 27," the woman said to the man, pointing at me. "He's getting fixed tomorrow." "Fixed"? Was I broken? Was Laura unhappy with me the way I was?

I will admit to you, dear reader, that my spirits were as low as spilled milk flattening on a grimy floor. I scraped at the shredded newspaper that lined my cell and crouched in the meager nest I'd made, waiting for I knew not what. The people left. The overhead lights went off. The room was lit only by a dim red square above the door.

The paper in the cage next to mine rustled and a black cat stuck his head up and looked at me. "Whatta ya in for?" he asked, in a rather familiar manner.

"I don't know to what you are referring," I answered him in all truthfulness.

"Hey Sylvester, get a load of this cat's syntax."

In the cell next to me an orange marmalade cat with an unfortunate pink nose looked me up and down. "I heard. Hoity-toity."

"Yeah, he's a fat cat for sure" came a voice from another cage.

"I'm sorry if I seem too well fed," I said. "But I'm quite furry by nature and I have big bones."

"Oh man, this I don't believe," said my black-furred neighbor.

"First time in, kid?" Sylvester asked me.

"I've never been here before, if that's what you mean. And I don't know what this place is or why I'm here. Sir."

"Man, you must be the politest cat in the joint," said the black cat. "Do you lap your cream from a silver spoon?"

"Mookie," said the orange cat with the porcine nose, "Give the kid a break. He's new."

"He's Newf? He's a Newfie?" an enormous black dog in a huge box across the room woofed out in a voice like truck brakes.

"Go stick your head in a lake," said Mookie. "He's a cat, you doofus. What's your name, cat?"

"Um . . . Robert?"

"So Bob, you say you don't know why you're here?"

"He's innocent," said a voice.

"That's what they all say," said another, and the room laughed.

"They watch too much television," said Sylvester. "Look, Robert, you're in the vet's holding pen. Veterinarian? Animal doctor? They're going to do something to you tomorrow, probably an operation. If it was just shots you'd be in and out. So, is there something wrong with you, a medical emergency?"

"Not that I know of." My voice quavered a little.

"You still got your nuts?" asked Mookie.

"Do you mean my testicles? Of course I do."

"That's probably it. And by tomorrow you probably won't."

"What?"

"They're gonna cut 'em off."

"They're what?!?"

"It's not so bad," put in Sylvester. "We've all been through it. Oh, you feel sad afterwards, unsettled. And there's the physical discomfort but that passes."

"But why? Why do they do this . . . this horrible thing?"

"Catacide, baby. They want to keep our tribe small. They're afraid of us. Used to burn us as witches." Mookie's eyes reflected the dim red light.

"We were also worshipped as gods," said Sylvester. "We hold the moon in our eyes, and we can look at kings."

"You ever seen a king, Vest-man?"

"I'm Rex!" yapped a tiny dog with blue bows in his fur. "I'm a king! I'm a king!"

"Good thing you got your cage to protect you, mosquito dog, or I would personally take you out," Mookie snarled.

The room erupted then, dogs barking and cats screeching back. Terrible things were said, insults and threats. I had never seen such behavior, heard such imprecations and abuse. My mind was a whirl – the world was a larger, rougher place than I had known; my testicles were going to be cut off; Laura had betrayed me; I was a hoity-toity cat. It was all too much for me. I began to scream. One by one the other animals fell silent, and still I screamed. It was as if the panic inside of me was trying to escape and all I could do was open my mouth and let the sound come out in ragged waves. Finally I stopped, trembling and exhausted.

"Poor kid. He's got the heebie-jeebies." Mookie surprised me with the kindness in his voice.

"Why? Why? Why?" I sobbed.

"They have to take away your wildness, son, or you wouldn't fit in an apartment." The big orange cat purred at me in a reassuring voice. "You get feelings you can't control if you're not cut. You yearn for things –"

"Puss puss puss," Mookie intoned, and then he moaned, as if bereft.

"You get wanderlust," Sylvester said. "You get so crazy with it you can jump out a window."

"That's right," said another voice. "My predecessor jumped from the thirteenth floor." Other voices chimed in, agreeing: "I knew a cat jumped from a moving car." "Found himself stuck on a window ledge." "Splat. Flat cat."

"Why? What are they looking for?" I asked.

There was a pause and then the voices chimed in again, soft and yearning: "The country." "Nature." "The real deal." "I was there once. A weekend." "I grew up on a farm." "I dream about it sometimes." "Mice. . ." " The voices drifted off.

A gloomy silence fell and I was left alone with my thoughts. I had not been with other cats since I was taken from my family, and I thought of them now: my slim beautiful mother, and my siblings, to whom I felt so close they were an extension of myself. I remembered the comfort of their bodies nestled next to mine. I remembered struggling to stand, to walk, and how at last we ventured from our mother's soothing warmth.

I remembered how we left the cardboard box, and ventured out upon hard-wood and carpet and beyond, to the vast shiny expanse of linoleum ringed with tall slick white boxes which we could not climb up. A makeshift plywood barrier prevented us from infiltrating the rooms beyond, but we soon breached that as well, a horde of furry barbarians climbing up each other and over the top.

I remembered a tall rectilinear object with a space underneath - a cre-denza, I know now - and under that we formed our clubhouse, my two sisters, three brothers and me. Oh happy days of wrestling and caterwauling, of shifting allegiances, battles and sweet sleep. The first bowl of milk (sneezing as the milk went up my nose). The first attempt to climb into the litter box. My first fur ball.

I remembered, with pain, when our mother first began to weary of us. She'd spend her time looking out the window and sometimes howled on full moon nights. She'd swat us when we tried to nurse.

"You're ruining my figure," she complained. "I used to be so slim and sleek."

Once she nipped me so sharply that I yelped and tried to scuttle under the cre-denza, but I was by now too big. You've heard the saying "Fierce As a Mother Cat"? Imag-ine my profound shock when my own mother no longer seemed ready to defend me with her life. She batted me away now from her breast, the former font of sustenance and love.

Then I remembered Laura. She too had cast me aside. My further thoughts that night are not worth dragging into the light. Eventually I fell asleep.

I was awakened by the sound of my cage door being opened. The room was brightly lit. A white rubber hand grabbed the scruff of my neck; another stabbed me with something thin and sharp. I tried to twist around and defend myself but my body didn't work right. I opened my mouth to bite but it turned into a yawn. I tumbled back into a dizzy sleep.

She'd Spend Her Time Looking Out The Window

I Had Become A Cat

When I awoke again Laura was stroking my head. I was so overjoyed to see her that I butted my head against her hand before I remembered that I was mad at her. I turned away. My body felt strange. There was a soreness between my legs, and an empty feeling there.

"He'll be groggy for a while; let him rest," said a voice.

Laura took me home. When she lifted me from the bag I was shaky as a kitten, and wanted to be alone. Laura carried me to the kitchen and offered chicken livers, but I had the strength of character to turn up my nose at them. I crawled under the sofa. I emerged at dusk, ravenous. I ate, then curled up underneath the bed. Laura called to me and finally I could resist no longer; I jumped up on the bed and nestled against her.

"Oh Bobster, I'm sorry," Laura said. Love sometimes means having to say you're sorry.

The days went by, the weeks, the months. I turned one year old, and Laura downshifted from Feline Growth to Feline Maintenance. My kitten fat – my big round tum – was gone. My legs were long, my tail a glorious plume of fur, my head was broad, my ruff and pantaloons were thick and plush. I had become a cat.

An Unwelcome Rival

As the year progressed I noticed a gradual change in Laura. She'd always had her pensive moods, like anyone, but they seemed to increase in frequency. She spent more time staring at horizons past the walls, unseen phantasms in her restless mind.

I endeavored to ease her moods by sitting in her lap, butting my head against hers, and in general weathering her melancholy with a mature solicitude. As a kitten I think I was not so sensitive to others' moods and needs; I had the blind solipsism of youth. Empathy is a painful burden, however; I felt for Laura but was helpless to affect the bedrock of her unhappiness. I became unhappy too, morose, a fussy eater. A dreary winter passed.

As spring approached there was a quickening, a change, and she began to sing. She stayed out late several times, and finally did not come home at all one night. I was beside myself. I slept fitfully at the foot of the bed, ears swiveling to every sound. At dawn I crept up to her pillow – redolent of her scent – and lay down there and fell into a sleep enlaced with dreams of things I'd lost: my mother's warmth and rasping tongue; the furry plums of my plump testicles; the rich, fat-laden taste of Feline Growth.

The key turned in the lock. In a flash I was downstairs at the door. She entered, bending down as always to pat my head – but there was someone with her. I sprang away. She did not come after me or inquire. "He's shy," she said, and turned into the stranger's arms.

Well, it got worse. Several nights later the creature was in our bed with her. They patted and caressed each other and Laura uttered sounds she'd never made with me. I jumped up on the bed, trying to distract her – and HE KICKED ME OFF. Shock, outrage and indignation coursed through my blood. I had to regain my rightful place. I grabbed my wire toy in my mouth and leapt back on the bed. This charming ploy had always pleased a crowd. This time SHE pushed me – gently, but decidedly – off.

Drastic measures were called for. I ran downstairs to the kitchen. I had been excavating the area under the sink for some time – one of my several ongoing projects, along with a graceful unfurling of the WELCOME mat edge and a discreet vertical pattern engraved upon the sofa arm. Now I dug under rusty rags and damp debris until I stuck gold: a large live water bug, frisky and sleek. My intention was to disarm Laura with this, my best, most irresistible toy. However going up the stairs proved difficult – it wriggled and slid from my mouth – and so I had to crunch it up a bit to slow it down.

There is an art to disabling one's prey without killing it. All I can say in my defense was that I was both overly anxious and inexperienced – this being my largest trophy heretofore. Reader, I murdered him. That is why, instead of interrupting her rompings with the interloper and welcoming me back with remorse and delight, Laura cried out in dismay and banished me from her bedroom – our bedroom – for the duration of that painful night.

Cats are adaptive creatures. As the interloper began spending almost every night with Laura, I began to spend nights on the sofa, coming onto Laura's side of the bed at dawn for a few hours of comfort. The interloper became a fixture, and I suffered his meager attempts at détente with cool civility. He didn't help matters by announcing, "I'm a dog man myself." A dog would have drooled on his pants and shredded his shoes, but maybe this is the kind of territorial overkill that men can identify with. I've noticed that packs of male humans seem very like dogs in their behavior, growling and showboating to establish dominance, expecting the females to expose their vulnerable throats. At least they have the virtue of being fairly transparent: what you see is what you get. Men. And dogs too, I imagine. Cats, I know, are accused of being devious, snooty and sly – by those who cannot appreciate subtlety and wit.

Speaking of wit: his was leaden at best. "Fetch me my slippers, Bob," he'd say, and guffaw as if he actually amused himself with this feeble puerility.

But as I say, we are adaptable, and I was willing to accommodate the presence of this chien-ophile as long as he didn't take too many liberties. What irked me, however, was how he treated Laura. At times he was distracted, distant, aloof. But when he was in the mood he would nuzzle up to her and purr endearments as if he had a perfect right to her affections. And she gave in, every time. She called him Henry, Hank, and a variety of twee variations I cannot bring myself to recollect.

A Cornucopia Of Birds

My Horizons Expand

❧ ❧

Another Journey

Spring sprang; the days grew long; the birds were in a frenzy in the ailanthus tree. Laura and the interloper seemed full of plans and secrets. One day I was carried back to the dreadful place that reeked of astringent smells and other animals' fear. I didn't see Mookie or Sylvester; the woman in white carried me to a private room where she stuck needles in my skin and performed other unmentionable indignities. Back home my head felt large and unwieldy, as if a giant hand were pressing me to earth. I crawled under the bed to sleep it off.

I woke to turmoil. Laura pulled out the suitcase where I had taken refuge, transferred me to the bed and started filling the suitcase with the contents of her bureau drawers. Cartons of books and papers came next, then boxes of shoes and hats and kitchen pots – a veritable pyramid of possessions rose next to the door. My known world was in confusion, flurry, and flux.

"Where are my slippers, Bob?" asked Hank, and in my mood I would have bitten his naked, furless feet, if I were not so dizzy.

The next day I was again stuffed in the nylon bag, protesting, yowling, scratching for escape. We went downstairs and out the door; we got into a big metal box, with sofas front and back. Henry turned a circle in his hands and we moved off down the street. Laura held my bag upon her lap. I could smell her through the mesh and hear her voice, a litany of reassuring sounds.

"This is a car," she said. "We're on the road. You'll like it when we get there."

I realized I would need my strength for whatever lay ahead, and so I slept, lulled by the motion, by the susurrations of the other cars, a sound like wind and rain, like breath. It seems my life is to be punctuated with journeys, I thought as I drifted off, with episodes of time lost, swaying in the nylon bag, echoes of the womb. I remember wondering if after this journey there would be a rebirth.

I woke up when motion stopped. It was night. Laura opened a door and stepped outside, bearing me aloft. The cool air felt like fragrant draughts of water bathing my nose in blissful benediction. That's hyperbolic and purple as an Easter egg, I know, but I was deranged with new sensations. The smells were so fresh and multifarious it was as if I'd never smelled before; I had lived in a world of olfactory deprivation. And sounds! The night was thick with clicks and chirrs, a myriad of tiny insect voices spinning a web of aural information.

All this I took in in a flash. I was carried up some steps, and through a door into a house. The night reverberated, a narrow, vivid corridor between the car and sill. Lights came on, my bag unzipped. We were in a house. Food, water,

The Dangerous
Unknown Of
Corners

the sand-filled box – the necessary alpha and omega of my digestive cycle – were shown to me, then I was left alone to explore while Laura and the interloping Hank lugged bags and boxes into every corner of the many-cornered house. There were two staircases, closets, pantries, hallways, and a full accouterment of furniture in every room. I sidled around the dangerous unknown of corners, inspecting under sofas for other quadrupeds, mapping out the refuges and escapes of my new territory. But all the while the unknown world outside the windows, a world I had been but briefly carried through, harried my imagination like a hunter stalking doomed prey. The black windows followed me like knowing eyes as I explored the house. The night was alive. It beckoned. It threatened. It waited.

I slept that night, for the first time, between Laura and Hank. The house seemed otherwise uninhabited, but there is safety in numbers and in the presence of benign creatures larger than oneself.

The World Is Animate

At dawn I was wide awakened by contentious voices.
"Hey! This is my branch!"
"Get off get off get off! Mine mine mine!"
"Find your own tree – "
"I was here first I was here first I was here first!"
Other voices joined in; a cacophony of calls cascaded through the morning air outside the house. I jumped off the bed, onto a sofa and looked through a window. From my window post in the city apartment I was familiar with pigeons, sparrows and the occasional intertwining pair of doves but here was a cornucopia of birds: sleek blue-gray birds with a cat-like call; a red bird with a pointy head; bright yellow birds with black wings and cap; and a huge black and white

A Paradise Beyond The Window Panes

bird who repeatedly smashed his head into a tree. What a panoply! And what squabbling!

"This is my twig, my branch, my tree, my meadow and my world – stay away! Stay away! For I am fierce and my beak is sharp, and I have work to do! I must call back the sun from the other side of night." I crouched on the window-sill, quivering, helpless with a dread desire. The light increased, the birdsong crested and ceased.

The sun rose and I saw a **a** paradise beyond the windowpanes, verdant and enticing. I wanted to get outside more than I have ever wanted anything. I jumped back on the bed and traversed the undulating form of my recumbent mistress. She stirred, groaned. I reached her head, and batted her face with a soft paw. She smiled and rubbed my head, then closed her eyes again. The interloper turned over, dragging most of the blankets with him, of course. I waited till I was sure he was asleep and then I pounced on Laura's hair.

"All right, all right." Laura rose alone (let sleeping dog lovers lie) and together we went downstairs and through the front door, into another world, a new dimension.

"Welcome to the country, Bob," said Laura. "Don't go too far."

The country! I remembered the talk of my old pals in the veterinary hold-ing pen. Sylvester and Mookie had spoken of the country like Ulysses's sailors yearning for home, and here I was.

There was a porch outside the door with steps down to a gravel path bisect-ing an expanse of verdant green. Bushes rose on either side. The porch itself was like a raft, a limbo land suspended between the linear world of angles and flat surfaces contained within the house, and the infinitely curveting universe beyond.

I took in this new experience one paw at a time, emerging from a land of shadows into sun, from black and white to Technicolor, from two dimensions into three.

Something suddenly pushed at me, an invisible force buffeting my whiskers and my tail. I whirled around, on guard, but there was nothing there. Laura laughed.

"That's wind, Bobcat," she said. Wind! I had never felt, heard, smelled wind before. It carried with it fragrances and messages from far away. Scents and sensibility bombarded me.

By nature I am not a "scaredy cat" but caution seemed a prudent course. I walked in ever widening arcs across the deck, returning at intervals to Laura, my ballast, my shoreline kept in sight. Laura watched me closely, and I was glad. In this way I explored the porch, up to the edge of the known world. Here be dragonflies, and grass, trees, bushes – a bewildering profusion of fecundity. Things moved and grew and smelled of growth and rot: flower fragrances as delicate as lace, leaf mold deconstructing into dirt. The world was animate and graced. And I – my very whiskers swiveled.

With every reflex poised I stepped down off the porch, onto the steps and to the ground. Underneath the porch was a wondrous dim cavern of stone stanchions, dirt, cobwebs, tantalizing dark smells, passageways that led back into abysmal depths. I took a few, hesitant steps forward.

"Bobcat!" Laura was crouching by the steps. "Don't go too far – come back!"

I pushed on towards the dark interior. The passageway narrowed; the ceiling lowered. Yet on I went, worming my way towards the secret heart of whatever mystery lay before me.

Suddenly I heard a chirring noise, and then a muffled voice: "Who's there? Get out – get out –." Loud rustling noises issued from the black beyond, as if

I Pounced On Everything

centuries of dead leaves were waking from their sleep, and a dark figure lurched towards me.

I shot into the sun and Laura's arms. She carried me inside, back to the safety and surfeit of civilization.

For those first days I dogged Laura's steps – if you'll pardon the expression – accompanying her from room to room until I grew familiar with my new domain. Laura let me outside several times a day and watched my progress, until she and I were confident that I had staked my claim. She began to leave me on my own, coming out at intervals and calling for me. I'd come. If anything, we grew closer; it felt as if we had a thin translucent thread attaching us. I located the window where she often sat and wrote; throughout my rambles I'd call up to her and she'd call down. Satisfied, I'd go on my way, exploring my astonishing new world.

This world was curvilinear; plants, rocks and sky eschewed straight lines. Everywhere I looked was a delicious confusion of pattern and line.

This world was animate. Wind blew, grass grew, and live things flew through air and crawled through foliage and field. There were black insects with jack-knifing hind legs; large mousy beasts with striped backs; birds that mocked me in my own voice; sculptural bright green insects like water bugs transformed and elevated into art; fat iridescent ground-crawling worms like animated bits of yarn; and honey-headed purple plants.I pounced on everything, lunging after crickets, chipmunks, catbirds, katydids, caterpillars, clover moving in the breeze.

And how marvelous it was to chew on grass! Why was there no grass in my apartment life? I would contemplate the tender confluence of stem and leaf, the gentle flanges of vibrant green before savoring each blissful bite. I rolled upon meadows of eat-

Frog

ables; I grazed like an herbivore, a veritable ungulate. My sturdy paws galloped cross the lawn, my tail a banner in the wind.

Every venture contained a milestone: ascending three feet up the honeysuckle bush, going to the stone wall and beyond, the first grasshopper, rain. (Water falling from the sky! A cat-unfriendly phenomenon, to be sure). Discovering a small pond, its dark surface dappled by tiny fish rising after insects; frogs leaping from the shore. They were too fast for me, but then I met a mouse who wasn't.

There were many mysteries. There was a large, muttering creature who lived under the house. The distant road was "bad." In the morning, grass was wet even if it hadn't rained. Outside at night was another No-Place-for-Cats. But the most astonishing thing to me was that my new world had no seeming end. Each day I defined a new perimeter; the next day's perambulations erased its boundaries.

Outside At Night Was Another No-Place-For-Cats.

I explored under the house on ginger paws. The large, muttering animal was ensconced in the black depths way under the house, its smell sour and strong. Occasionally I'd hear it chirring and muttering but I was wary of getting close enough to make out what it was saying. I saw the creature once at dusk, trundling away from the refuge of the porch. It looked like me only bigger. Its face was sharp, with a stripe across it, and stripes ringed its tail. This animal appeared to be light on its paws, despite its bulk. It sat up, bobbing and weaving in a very un-catlike way, and I saw that its paws were like small black hands. It examined the ground minutely, sticking these hands into everything – the compost heap, the fishpond, under rocks, between the stacked logs of the woodpile.

"Oh look, there's a raccoon!" Laura cried. It sat up and looked at us, then shook its head and glided back under the house.

"It looks perfectly healthy, but let's not tell Hank – you know how men are," Laura said to me, as if I would have anything to say to him. I kept my distance from the Fido-phile.

Hank pretty much ignored me too, although sometimes he would inflict his tiresome wit on me: "Here boy," he'd drag out like stale kat kibble, "fetch me my slippers, Bob." I suffered graciously, distant but polite. What did she see in him?

The only good thing about Hank was that he went away. After two days Laura would drive off with him in the car and come back alone, and for the next five days she and I would be blissfully alone together. But then he'd turn up again and monopolize Laura's attention and try his waggish ways on me, throwing sticks across the lawn and telling me to "go fetch," if you can imagine.

A Pathetically Small Dead Fish

Transfixed By Moths

The only interesting thing about Hank was that he sometimes arose at dawn and enacted a strange ritual. He'd pull on rubber boots that reached his armpits; don a vest festooned with pockets and a hat resembling a soft, inverted water dish – both bristling with feather insects on sharp hooks (I know, I pounced on one); take up nets and poles, cudgels and creels and set off on what he called "an expedition." He would return hours later with nothing to show for his efforts but a disagreeably damp appearance. Once, oh joy of joys, he came bounding over the lawn brandishing a pathetically small dead fish, of which he was inordinately proud. And do you think he thought to share his prey with me? Of course not. I was civility itself, however, and continued to thoughtfully array my hunting successes along the doorstep for his delectation.

Laura called me in each dusk, and after satisfying my hunger and my thirst I'd sit upon the windowsill, transfixed by moths. They were my steady, bread and butter prey. Their powdery crisp wings; the furry bodies juicy and plump as flying kiwi fruit; the pathos of their broken fluttering after the first hard swat – it moved me utterly; I reveled in their lingering demise.

I Found Myself In A Dark Wood

Out at Night – Adventure and Misadventure

৯ ২

Mice!

Laura did not let me out past dusk, but one night I escaped out the kitchen door when Hank carried the garbage to the outside bins. I admit I felt a thrill of naughty pleasure when I envisioned Laura scolding Hank for his inattention, and how she would spurn him while anxiously awaiting my return. Of course gloating goeth before a fall; mine boomeranged back in my furry face, as you shall soon see. I almost became a palpable embodiment of that old canard about curiosity and my kind.

I slipped between Hank's legs into the night. The full moon's light fell in broad bright swathes, strewing shadows like obsidian chips against the rocks and fields, turning the by now familiar world outside into a realm of alien enchantment. You've heard that cats can see at night. True, but it's the strange vision of a dream. Shades of grey verge into black. Perspective is skewed, flattened out. Everything seems out of kilter, off balance.

I was strangely agitated. I felt awake beyond the normal scope of wakefulness, with every nerve and follicle alert. As I skirted a shagbark hickory, I heard a small dry sound in the leaves and pounced, trapping a meadow mouse between my paws. It screamed once, its blunt-nosed face stretched wide in a rictus of terror. I lifted a paw and let it slip away, and then I pounced again. This time I hooked it in my claws and flipped it in the air, then batted it across the lawn before I broke its back with one last pounce and bit off its head.

Gentle reader, I will not falsely obsecrate your pardon for my seeming cruelty. Protracted enjoyment of the antics of our prey is in our feline natures; I cannot fight against the tide of blood and history. And from what I have observed on television, humans also have their inexplicable dark side. We are all animals under the skin.

"Bobcat! Bobcat!" Laura called for me. I saw her in the lighted kitchen window, and then she came outside and stood by the door. She was rattling my food dish before her like a talisman. I found her action both poignant and quite funny. As if pebbles of desiccated fish offal could lure me from live prey. I crouched in the shadows. Laura began walking, calling my name and shaking my food bowl. She crossed in front of me, and it was delicious to hide, cowering in mock fear. A mouse bolted at Laura's approach and I could not keep from lunging after it.

"There you are! Come on, let's go inside."

I let her rub my head, but when she tried to pick me up I twisted from her hands. The mice, the moon were calling me. A leaf rustled - a thrilling sound - and I leapt to investigate. Laura came after me but I danced just beyond her reach.

"Oh give the mice a rest!" she cried out in exasperation. "Haven't you killed enough rodents for today?" This seemed to me an astonishing question; how can you have too much of a good thing? It stopped me in my tracks, and Laura swooped down on me.

Forbearing reader, I growled at her. And worse: I showed my teeth. I am not proud of this. A lesser cat might plead in his defense that the moon made him do it, the smell of mice or the restless wind. All I can say is that another, atavistic cat surged through me and snapped at Laura as if with saber teeth. I was possessed, a channel for an ancestral beast that took no prisoners. Laura stepped back, hand at her throat. I felt a twinge of remorse, but swatted it away like a gnat. Let her know her place – and mine: outside, in the hunting fields. I didn't have to come when called. Killed enough rodents? I had just begun.

I jumped over the stone wall by the garden and ran into the field beyond. I heard Laura call but I moved on, through passages of shadow and light. Laura's voice wavered and stopped, and I put her from my mind. I sprang into the night sky, rejoicing in my strength, uncoiling the sinews of my mighty thighs.

The field beyond the house rustled with the scampering of tiny feet. There were mice everywhere, running through tunnels of dry grass. Wherever I turned, rodents ran rampant, triggering my deepest instincts to seek warm blood and flesh. Female mice go boldly across open fields while males scurry next to cover; each sex offers its own peculiar pleasures of the hunt. I became maddened with the plentitude; I stopped eating the crunchy heads, the succulent entrails, and killed only to kill. A veritable elation of killing took hold. The moon scudded through dark waves of clouds, and I knew myself no longer.

The Long Night Begins

In the middle of the night I found myself in a dark wood, dazed with the carnage I had caused. Blood and bits of fur bespattered my mouth and coat; the blood was singing in my ears. A disembodied pink, clawed foot lay upon the forest floor, a tiny kick of remorse. The horror! The horror!

The moon had slid into a far quadrant of the sky and the world was still. It was like waking into a dream. Huge trees, gnarled and serpentine, rose above me, their branches enlaced into a canopy of black. Between their trunks the forest offered a hundred pathways to unknown destinations. I had no memory of how I got there, or where home was – that safe box containing light, warmth, Laura's tender voice and bed.

Laura. I remembered her soft touch, and then remembered our last encounter. I had growled; I had shown my teeth. I had turned on her, and run away. Even if I could find my way back home, she wouldn't want me now. The night was vast, amorphous, alien. I was separate from it and afraid.

I began to walk – what else was there for me to do? And as I walked I became part of it. I became a creature of the night, of blood, wind, and growing things. The lighted house faded from my mind as I walked forth on pathways of the forest's whim. My muscles rippled underneath my fur and I exulted in my strength, my stealth, my expanded sense of self. I felt enormous and invincible. I could find food and resting spots at will. Anywhere I placed my massive paws was home. The world was my litter box.

I walked on. Creatures rustled and squeaked on all sides, but I was sated. A cat who walks by itself does not kill for sport. The slaughter of the mice was the unfortunate excess of an apartment-raised tyro. A true carnivore, a forest master, only kills to eat. The forest rose and fell as I traversed gullies and hills, streambeds and slopes, copses of beech trees, fern-glutted glens, and ridges fragrant with the scent of balsam firs.

The Full Moon Is The Time
For The Female Cat Ceremony

I heard a sound, so faint it was like a wisp of fragrance weaving through the wind, a lacewing fly against my whiskers. It was a sound unlike any I had heard before, yet I knew it, I knew it in my bones and blood. As if on their own volition my paws led me towards this siren song. Trees thinned out to bushes and scrub pines, and I emerged into a highland meadow palely lit by starlight and a hidden moon. The eerie sound was stronger now, a concatenation of ululating voices drawing me onwards.

Over the crest of a bracken tufted hill I came upon an astonishing sight. A circle of cats surrounded one solitary cat and all were yowling at the moon. The cat in the center was slight and three-colored – calico coins strewn on white fur. The eight cats ringed round were larger, and as I drew nearer I could see that some had torn ears or battered faces. Their eyes were closed, their noble heads thrown back and from their throats issued forth gorgeous spiraling cataracts of sound. I had never heard anything so achingly beautiful; you would have had to tie me with a thousand collars and deafen me with ear mites to keep me from this sound. Down

Calico Coins Strewn On White Fur

the hill I rushed, eager to join in. Seeing me, the cat in the center ceased her cater-wauls. One by one the singers stopped. The largest cat swiveled to face me.

"Who disturbs the ceremony? Are you one of us?"

"One of us? One of us?" echoed the others.

I had not seen others of my tribe since my surgical ordeal. "One of you," I said, perhaps too ardently.

"He looks too soft."

"His voice is high."

"His ears are innocent of war."

I did not feel so enormous now, nor so invincible.

The cat in the center moaned, an urgent, almost painful sound. "Hurry up," she hissed. "It's time, it's time."

I heard her voice and it all fell into place. I remembered my mother, pressing against the window in an anguish of desire. I thought of Laura, rolling in the bed with Hank. I remembered the talk of my caged compadres. This was a realm of the senses now barred to me.

I turned to flee but the others, the warrior males, jumped on me and threw me to the ground. Teeth seized my neck; hind feet rained blows on my belly and back; claws raked my thick fur. Fear filled my head, pushing out thought, resistance, flight. I gave up, reduced from forest master to frightened mouser. The largest cat pushed through the mob, cuffing the others aside. He smacked my face, but his claws were sheathed.

"Un-cat," he spat. "Go back to your soft life, go back to the humans who took your power from you. Un-cat. Lap pussy. Fraud. Fake. Thing."

The other cats took up the chorus: "Un-cat. Fraud. Thing. Run, pussy, run.

Flight

I ran. Branches, briars and brambles impeded my wild flight, but headlong I ran deep into the woods. Stones, streams and fallen trees directed my trajectory like fingers pointing crazily in all directions. This way, now this, turn here, veer here – I ran from the hideous screeching of their jeers.

When I stopped the woods were dark and still. They no longer felt like home, their endlessness no longer made me bold. A dread anxiety filled me instead. I wanted a wall, a corner, something flat and orderly. I wanted Laura. What had she done to me? Taken from me? I didn't care. I wanted her. Then I remembered that she no longer wanted me, wild cat ingrate that I was. I was alone in all the world. I looked around and the world all looked the same, trees and more trees, shades of grey and black in endless repetition. I cried then, a small and inadvertent mew.

A huge, ghostly shape plummeted through the trees. I felt the wind of its vast wings and recoiled just as its talons sliced the air inches from my head. The thing wheeled and came back. I lurched against a fallen log, which gave way beneath me – its center rotted out. I scrambled back into the hollow bole. The creature swept past me again, its eyes flat disks of light. Claws scraped against the thin wood over my head. My mouth opened independent of volition, stretched wide in frozen terror . . .

I jammed myself as far back into the log as I could. The smell of fungus and rot was overpowering, a palpable sensation in my nose, but I didn't dare stick even a whisker out. I forced myself to stay still, to endure the slithering things

I Felt The Wind Of Its Vast Wings

"Come Closer Kitty."

exploring my fur. I ached with fear, catatonic. My throat hurt with the effort not to cry. I dared not even purr for consolation.

I must have slept, because the next thing I remember was a thin grey light defining the ragged mouth of the log, and the first bird rousing to greet the dawn. I was in agony from lying in such confinement. I crawled to the entrance, ventured a paw outside and snatched it back. No waiting wings swept down on me. Inch by inch I emerged from my shelter, my protective shell. I stretched, normally a deep pleasure, but now a quick necessity. I ached from the pummeling I'd received. Hunger yawned in my belly.

I looked around. The forest was shrouded in mist, eldritch and mysterious. Where was my home? I'd heard birds talk of resonating with the earth's magnetic fields to find their way. I stood still and tried to fix on a directional pull, but all I felt was hunger, cold, and damp. I chose a direction with a dispassion verging on inertia and started walking on the forest floor's moist duff. It was like treading on a vast, dank sponge. Shapes loomed and trembled in the mist before resolving into trees. Bushes pretended to be bears. Branches rubbed against each other like chuckling wolves. My paws were sore but I kept walking, stupid with misery.

Time passed. One by one birds overlapped their voices. The sky grew lighter, the mist thinned. Suddenly a bush to my left transformed into a real raccoon – the same hunched shape as the one who lived under our house, but otherwise a stranger to me: larger and somehow shabbier.

"Kitty," he said, startling me out of the stupor of unhappiness. "Big tailed kitty. Tail like mine. Dark paws too. Come closer kitty." I sat down, wary. "Don't be afraid. What's kitty doing out here in the woods?"

"I am going for a walk."

"By yourself? So far from the dwellings of men? But perhaps you are a forest kitty – come close and let me look at you."

"Where are they, the dwellings of men?"

"Why does kitty want to know?" He didn't want to tell me but his eyes glanced left. His tail twitched, a semaphore of danger.

"I'm hungry," I allowed.

"I'm hungry too. Yes, sometimes it's easy to find food near humans. And perhaps, kitty, they'll let you inside."

"Perhaps."

"Perhaps I'll take you there – if you're nice to me."

"How do you mean?"

"Come closer kitty, come close and I'll tell you. Don't be afraid. I'll help you; I'll take you to where the human houses are. All you have to do – come close and let me whisper in your ear –" and then he sprang at me, his eyes like deranged moons, spittles of foam between his needle teeth.

I jumped back, my heart surging with terror. The raccoon stumbled, and I saw that he was unsteady on his feet.

"Kitty. Naughty Kitty. Come here. Let me bite you; it will be so pleasant, so delicious for us both."

He took a swaying step towards me. I arched my back and hissed, my fur on end.

"Ooh, big kitty. Big brave kitty." He lunged at me again, his face contorted to a demon mask. I reared back, turned and ran. He came after me; I could hear him following like a nightmare beast. I ran. When I could run no more I trotted, then I walked. He was no longer behind me but in the misty light I saw him in every bush, every rustle of wind. I veered to the left, towards the dwellings of men.

I came to a road. The day was well advanced by now, as was my hunger. I followed the road till it led past a house. A little boy was pitching pebbles at a tree. He saw me and picked up a rock. I was so astonished I didn't think to run until I saw his arm snap forward. I bolted, but the rock caught me on the haunch in a bursting star of pain. I ducked under a spreading bramble bush and crawled through its labyrinth of branches. I could hear the boy's feet breaking twigs as he tried to get at me. I crawled out the other side, onto a ragged lawn, jagged with panic. Reality was tipping over.

In the distance I saw a field of high green plants in rows. Ran towards it. A man in coveralls and a peculiar hat was riding a tall, red, rackety car between the tasseled stalks. I recognized ears of corn, but they were attached to the plants, not on plates. The man saw me and stopped his noisy machine.

"Help!" I cried, even though I knew he couldn't understand me.

He turned his face and yelled: "Sic 'em, boy! Get that cat!"

A white blur exploded at the edge of sight. I heard deep barks like metal being ripped. My feet flew. I dove into the green wall of corn, down first one row then another. Crows wheeled overhead, a screaming arc. Mice skittered from my path. Hip hurt. Dog crashed through stalks, a pulpy, tearing sound. The pounding of my heart took up the universe, my lungs grabbed at my throat for air.

Ran to the cornfield's edge, a road. Cars roaring by. While at my back, hurrying near, the hound of hell I heard. His hot breath scorched my neck. I streaked across the black tar. Brakes squealed – a car missed me by inches. Heard

Dog Crashed Through Corn Stalks

a car door open, slam. I catapulted through a brake of rushes – and fell in the ditch on the far side. The smell, the sound and the feeling of wet assaulted me: the ditch was full of water and I was swimming.

The white dog churned himself into furious speed, rushing among the reeds with open jaws and lashing tail. He plunged in after me, biting the water trying to get at me. Retribution, swift vengeance, eternal malice were in his whole aspect, and spite of all that mortal cat could do, the solid white buttress of his forehead smote my starboard flank. My claws scored his face, glancing harpoons. The white behemoth drew back an instant, surprised.

I scrambled up the other shore, panting, heart bursting, pain raking up my leg. The white beast came on, breeching from the roiling waters. My fur was sodden, a deadly weight. In the distance were trees I knew I'd never reach. Teeth bared, I turned to face my death, that final harbor, from whence I'd unmoor no more –

"Hey! Hey!" A man flung himself into the ditch, grappling with the dog. I jerked myself away and staggered up the embankment, beyond thought or cognition. Moving, keep moving –

"Bobcat! Bobcat!"

I wobbled around. It was Hank, lanky and lunky as ever, his voice fraught, his clothes sopping, a piece of cattail hanging from his ear. He held on to the wet dog with both hands. We all three stood still, panting hard. Slowly Hank crouched down and looked the dog full in the face.

"Bad dog. You are a very very BAD DOG. Now go home. Go home." The dog wagged his tail, as if this had been a jolly romp. His tongue lolled insolently over his sharp teeth. He barked once – "What a devilish rogue I am!" – then he trotted back across the road and disappeared into the corn.

Hank swung around to me, held out his hand. "Bobcat – it's me. Here boy, don't be scared. Please – "

I let him pick me up. I had no strength left to run or resist. Hank put his face against my fur, my bedraggled, matted, stinky fur.

"Where have you been?" he asked. "We've been so worried."

"We"? My heart flared; maybe Laura had forgiven me. Hank carried me to the car and drove me home.

He Held On To The Dog With Wet Hands

For Once, He Was At A Loss For Words

Home Is The Prodigal

Laura cried when she saw me, and cried again when she saw the welt on my hip. I was made much of; fed and combed, scolded and cosseted. After I ate, I crawled onto bed and slept a sleep deeper than dreams.

When I awoke it was dark. My food bowl was calling to me. I padded downstairs. As I passed the living room, I saw Hank sitting under a light with a book in his lap. Halfway down the hall I looped back, entered the living room and glided up against his legs. Hank reached down and scratched my head and rumpled my ears.

"Hey Bob, fetch me my slippers buddy." He burnished this old chestnut once again, but this time I found it nearly endearing. I climbed back up the stairs to the bedroom. It was short work to bat and prod his ratty slippers from their spot beside the bed to the head of the stairs; a final push sent them thumping down the steps.

"What the – ?" Hank came out of the living room. I sashayed down the steps and stood next to his slippers, looking up at him. For once, he was at a loss for words.

I left Hank scratching his head and glided into the kitchen. Laura was there, washing the dishes. I stopped, and we looked at each other.

"Well look who's here. Jungle Bob."

I looked away. A cat may look at a king, perhaps, but I admit I was abashed and could not meet my Laura's gaze.

"So. Why did you growl at me? Why did you run away? What were you thinking of? Did you think you were a wild cat, a real bobcat?"

I hung my head.

"I was up all night calling for you. I thought something terrible had happened to you. The woods at night is no place for a small cat."

I shuffled my paws, feeling very small indeed. I raised my face and looked at her, trying to convey how sorry I was. The kitchen clock ticked loudly.

"Oh Bobster." Laura picked me up and held me to her bosom. I allowed the liberty, wet soapy hands and all; I welcomed it. I butted my abject head against her shoulder in a mute appeal for forgiveness.

"Oh Bob," she said, "my little mugwumpuss. I missed you so much."

Laura kissed the top of my head and I purred against her cheek and we had a tender reconciliatory scene that would have made Louisa May Alcott blush.

"So – are you ready for a little more fatted calf?" she finally asked, and I responded enthusiastically with affirmative sweeps of my tail.

Forgiven, loved and fed – life's hardships make sweeter its rewards.

Forgiven

How many of my allotted lives I may have lost on my misadventure does not bear thinking about. I am resolved to cherish the remaining span. Prudence dictates that I relinquish any conceit of myself as a cat who walks by himself. All that falderal about "the wide world over is my home" was so much youthful swagger. Instinct is a beautiful thing – in moderation. It is a mark of maturity and wisdom, I believe, to be content with one's place in the great scheme of things. Youth must have its vaunted fling but I am now a quite contented cat.

The simple, yet elegantly subtle truth is that I am an in-between cat. I am drawn to the siren song of nature, red in proverbial tooth and claw, but resist casting off all ties to the dwellings of men. I float between two worlds, just like the porch, that raft which juts into the great green world, yet is moored to the bedrock of the house.

The raccoon still lives under the house. He is saner, I hope and believe, than the creature I encountered in the deep woods, but I give him a wide berth nonetheless. He is a constant reminder of his unfortunate cousin, nature gone awry. Mr. Rochester had a madwoman in the attic to remind him of youthful folly and the cruel caprices of nature; I have my raccoon in the basement. Sometimes at dusk I hear him muttering to himself as he trundles across the lawn. I see him reaching his paws into dark corners, turning things over, and then he disappears into the gloaming.

Life does have shadows, true, but on the whole my own life is pleasing and complete. At this very moment Laura is in the kitchen, singing as she cooks – chicken livers sizzling in sweet butter. The scent floats upon the summer breeze like a charming melody. Hank is mowing the lawn, stirring up grasshoppers for my imminent delectation. He is a reliable buffer zone against bad dogs, and not such a bad duffer himself, once you get to know him. I myself am purring on the glider on the porch, gazing with an anticipatory gleam at grasshoppers hopping on a bed of greens. I'll attend to them presently, just as soon as I've had another short nap and prolonged stretch in the delicious, lucent sunshine of this perfect day in this best of all possible worlds.

FINIS

The Best Of All Possible Worlds.

KATHERINE BURGER'S plays have been produced in the United States, London, Paris and Berlin. She wrote and illustrated "Animal ABC's," for children, and has illustrated two books of poetry written by her mother Otis Kidwell Burger: "Cats, Love & Other Surprises," and "Love Is A Season" [published by Dr. Cicero Press]; all are available on Amazon. Katherine's artwork is primarily collage. She has sold her work privately and exibited in various galleries. Some of her artwork is available as greeting cards at bobcatbooksandcards.com. A portion of all sales is donated to organizations which benefit animals and the environment. Katherine lives in the Hudson Valley with her husband and their two indoor cats.

Afterward

❧ ❧

Anumber of years ago, four days after Christmas, I put one of the great loves of my life to sleep. I'd seen him come into this world and witnessed his leaving it. I pressed my face against his furry forehead one last time, then stepped back to let the vet administer the sedative, then the medication that stopped his heart. And just like that the constant companion for one third of my life was gone.

When I turned 40 I'd been single – and increasingly disheartened about it – for a long time. I was living in New York City, temping at investment banks, not having much luck with my writing, and performing intermittently with an off-off Broadway theater company. Let my life change, I pleaded with the candles on the cake – bring me change, bring me happiness, bring me love.

I went to an art colony in Vermont and fell in love with that enchanted landscape. I met a man there, a fellow playwright, and wanted so much for my life to now be about Vermont and having a partner that I moved from New

York City to be with him, bringing Roxy, my skittish orange cat. The man had invited me to come, but in retrospect I can admit that the pressure of how much I wanted this may have forced his hand. Yes, there were connections between us, but it was an unbalanced and bruising relationship.

Two springs later Roxy drowned in the Winooski River, her paw caught in her collar. I was bereft. We borrowed a pregnant farm cat from the local dairy farmer and she gave birth in July to six disparate kittens. One was a dark fluffy male, a tiny Steiff toy, who one day climbed determinedly up my pants leg and onto my lap, where he fell into a deep and trusting sleep. I had a physical sensation of my heart opening, a bond forming. We kept him, and found homes for the other kittens.

That fall the man and I endured a difficult break-up. I moved back to New York; he got Vermont, but I got Bobcat. I named him that because as he grew larger his swirled markings, tufted ears and luxuriant fur revealed him to be a lynx-in-training. He clearly had Maine Coon in him, although he was smaller, and his face didn't have the jutting, canine-like muzzle of some Maine Coons. He had a wide face, with the classic tabby "M" above his golden green eyes, and dark stripes radiating out from their corners. He grew a massive leonine ruff and his tail became a cascading plume. His coat was a brindle of brownish stripes, tipped with black; his belly fur a plush cream; his legs marked with wide black chevrons. His coat was so long and thick that he looked like a miniature musk ox, long fur sweeping over short and sturdy legs, tufts of snow-defying fur sprouting between the pads of his big paws. He was gorgeous.

The next few years were difficult. I had injured my dominant hand, and after several misdiagnoses and scary months of escalating pain and not being able to type for money or myself, I found a hand specialist who recognized that I'd torn a tendon. I was still wearing a cast from the surgery to repair it when I was diagnosed with endometrial cancer. I must have known subliminally that I was ill; I'd started a new play shortly before my diagnosis that I thought was going to be a snappy rom-com, but found myself writing a completely different play in which one of the characters gets cancer and dies. I had a complete hysterectomy, and lived. Family and friends rallied, and I had Bob. I was in bed a lot then, recuperating, and Bob was a reliable solace, a responsive, interactive being. He'd lie on top of me, belly to belly, in an ecstasy of rubbing his head and chin against my hand and looking at me with his steady, golden green gaze.

I kept in touch with people in Vermont. A friend's young male dog died unexpectedly, and when another friend turned down a social engagement to be with her, someone scoffed about "sitting shiva for a dog." But I understood. Being alone can be liberating and wonderful, but there can also be a constant penumbra of loneliness, and for these two women their dogs offered not just companionship and the proverbial unconditional love, but connection to a masculine energy. Bob was the masculine energy in my life. Even fixed, he exuded a jaunty, self-confident, very male aura. Aside from a few intermittent dates, Bob remained the closest male energy in my life for the next seven years.

Eventually, my birthday wish was granted: my post-Vermont life manifested a series of gratifying changes. The play I'd written had productions in Los Angeles, London, Paris, Berlin and Westport, Connecticut (on opening night Paul Newman kissed my hand!). I landed two interesting jobs: in the winter I wrangled the child performers at the Metropolitan Opera; and in the summer I directed an artists' residence program at an art colony in The Hudson Valley.

Bob, of course, came with me. I introduced him to the outdoors very cautiously, monitoring his widening excursions until he was clearly at home and reveling in this new green world. Maine Coons are famously social, and Bob loved being the colony cat. He greeted new residents, paid studio visits, attended the open studio parties, and took his place on the dinner table bench on the porch, never grabbing for food, but simply hanging out with us, alert and interested – although not averse to a bit of chicken slipped under the table. And he was our muse: artists drew and photographed him; there was a Bob poem; I wrote this novella inspired by him. Even residents who said they didn't particularly grok cats conceded that he was an especially endearing animal. He was friendly to everyone – except veterinarians – but he and I were clearly each other's creatures. He knew the sound of my car and came bounding up to greet it. He insisted on being on my lap if I was at the computer, or on the big table if I was working in my art studio. He slept in the crook of my knees each night.

He had to learn to share me, however, first with another cat. Celeste was one of an abandoned litter and I hoped she would be company for Bob while I spent long hours at the Met. It took time, but they became companionable, if not enamored of each other. Celeste was at first something of an auxiliary cat, she who walks by herself. But even as her sweet, goofy personality blossomed, Bob was still the alpha cat. I'd grown up with cats; as an adult I'd had Priscilla and then Roxy, but Bob was my guy.

Then Bob had a bigger challenge: I met Randy. Randy came to the colony for a writing residency. The first thing I noticed about him was his pale blue eyes, wolf's eyes. And he was tall. And smart. Kind. Wry. Musical. Liked to hike. Said he liked cats. Although much later he told me that he saw Bob as a rival at first, and was perturbed that I called Bob "my guy." But as Randy became my guy, he and Bob reached a détente, which grew eventually to love. Bob began greeting Randy at the door of our cabin as well, and shared evening lap-time on the couch with both of us.

And it was Randy who one winter noticed that Bob seemed uncomfortable using the litter box and insisted we take him to the vet, where he was diagnosed with lymphoma. The vet called in the middle of surgery to say he had taken out what tumors he could and that we had a choice of trying chemotherapy, which would be expensive but might give Bob a few more months of life, or having him put to sleep now. I couldn't bear the thought of losing him so abruptly, so I embarked on what was indeed a costly effort to stabilize Bobcat's health. At one point he had four doctors: his vet and an oncologist in New York City; his vet upstate; and an alternative vet who administered acupuncture and flower essences. Over time he developed kidney, heart and thyroid conditions; he endured blood tests, x-rays, and an evolving regimen of medications and prescription food. He could be grumpy and irascible, but Bob bore everything with good grace.

Bobcat confounded all expectations and lived another five years, good years. He still had an avid interest in food, in socializing, in moths and mice. He still trotted beside me every morning from our cabin down to the colony's main lodge and put in his time as the colony cat. He still presided over dinner parties in our New York apartment. He became more and more affectionate, insisting now on sleeping in my arms every night, pressed against my breastbone like a purring teddy bear and pushing his head against mine. He got thinner. His resplendent tail and coat got thinner. As his coat got patchier his short little musk ox legs were revealed to be long and thin, the bones visible. His entire skeleton was palpable. What a narrow pelvis he had after all, how fragile his ribcage was, a flexible comb of bones. Only his face was still broad and beautiful. In his glorious prime Bob weighed over ten pounds; now he was less than five, a skinny squirrel in my arms. But he was still affectionate, still eating, not suffering.

But then it became clear that he was going into a steep decline and we made the wrenching decision to have him eased him from this world. Afterwards Randy and I wept. We stopped at a bar on the way home to raise a glass to Bob's memory. He was 19½, a long life for any cat. He was a constant, loving and healing presence for much of my adult life, a companionable, complicated, endearing being who was the bridge between an unhappy relationship, and the man I'm now married to. I wish Bob could have been at the wedding. He always loved a party.

Requiescat, my Bobcat.

ACKNOWLEDGMENTS

જ જ

The author would like to thank Carey Harrison for his friendship and support of this project; Abigail Sturges for designing this book with such artistry; and Randy Burgess for editing the manuscript with empathy and expertise.

New fiction from Dr. Cicero Books, available on Amazon:

THE WORK OF THE HEART by Robert Kelly
Reading him "is to accompany the author on a walk whose only destination is under the sign: Keep your eyes open and pay attention." —John Yau

JOHNNY ALLAN BY John M. Keller
A timeless and topical read —*Booklist*
Reminiscent of Fitzgerald. —*World Literature Today*

THE LOST TRAVELLER BY Steve Wilson
There's a writer here, beneath the blood-boltered leather.
—*Martin Amis*
Thoughtful, funny, savage and sexy. —*Time Out*

TIGER BY Ashley Mayne
Mayne's prose is ferocious and lovely. This is a haunting story that confronts the spaces in which violence and beauty meet.
—*Foreword Reviews*

ASMITA BY Seneka Aberyratne
Abeyratne's command of prose is technically brilliant. *Asmita* is a timely criticism of a cross-section of Sri Lankan society.
—*Sri Lanka Daily News*

HOW TO PUSH THROUGH BY Carey Harrison
As thorough an examination of postwar European consciousness as Thomas Mann's *The Magic Mountain* was of its era
—*American Library Journal*

 For more, visit *drcicerobooks.com*

To the memory of my beloved mentor, the distinguished Brazilian educator, Dr. Emanuel Cicero, born in 1907 in Ubatuba, São Paulo. Rector of the College of Rio Grande do Sul from 1943 to 1978, he died in 1988 in Lisbon.

Maximiliano Reyes, publisher

-FIM-

Dr. Cicero Books